"Go and make disciples of all nations, baptizing them in the name of the Father and of the Son and of the Holy Spirit, and teaching them to obey all that I have commanded you" (Matt. 28:19–20).

The Great Commission encompasses the whole task of the church. And here is help for fulfilling that task—the DISCIPLING RESOURCES series. Designed for small-group use, whether Bible study, Sunday school, or fellowship groups, this effective approach is firmly based on biblical principles of disciple building.

Each group member receives his or her own copy of the book, which guides the group through thirteen weekly meetings. Every step of the group- and personal-study process is included, plus biblical material and commentary. Leaders need only facilitate participation. This series is designed to increase knowledge of God's Word, cultivate supportive personal relationships, and stimulate spiritual growth—an adventure in being His disciples.

Titles in this exciting new series:

Available now	Projected
Basic Christian Values	*Being Christ's Church (Ephesians)*
First Steps for New and Used Christians	*Discipling Your Emotions*
	Developing Personal Responsibility
Fruit of the Spirit	*A Life of Fellowship (1 John)*
The Good Life (Rom. 12–16)	

THE GOOD LIFE

A STUDY OF ROMANS 12-16

LARRY RICHARDS
NORM WAKEFIELD

ZONDERVAN
PUBLISHING HOUSE

OF THE ZONDERVAN CORPORATION
GRAND RAPIDS, MICHIGAN 49506

THE GOOD LIFE
© 1981 by The Zondervan Corporation

Library of Congress Cataloging in Publication Data

Richards, Lawrence O
    The good life.

    (Discipling resources)
    1. Bible. N.T. Romans XII-XVI—Study. 2. Christian life—
Biblical teaching—Study and teaching. I. Wakefield, Norm, joint
author. II. Title. III. Series.

BS2665.5.R49   227'.106   80-27939
ISBN 0-310-43431-9

Scripture passages are from the Holy Bible: New International
Version. Copyright © 1978 by the New York International Bible
Society. Used by permission.

Edited by Mary Bombara

Printed in the United States of America

CONTENTS

GOOD NEWS

Romans 12:1–2

Many philosophers
have asked,
"What is
the Good Life?"
The apostle Paul
in Romans 12
begins with
a distinctive statement,
and with
"Good" News.

BEGIN TOGETHER

God's good is not abstract ideas or concepts. God's *true goodness* has a great and wonderful impact on *life.*

Look at the verses that begin our study, Romans 12:1 and 2. Then look at the next page, where the good (being a living sacrifice, holy, pleasing God, etc.) is shown, together with its impact on our lives.

Think together, and in the spaces provided write as many descriptive words or phrases as you can that tell what a life *without* God's goodness will be like. Choose things which are opposite from, or reflect the lack of, the qualities stated in the passage. To help you get started, examples are included.

Therefore, I urge you, brothers, in view of God's mercy, to offer your bodies as living sacrifices, holy and pleasing to God—which is your spiritual worship. Do not conform any longer to the pattern of this world, but be transformed by the renewing of your mind. Then you will be able to test and approve what God's will is—his good, pleasing and perfect will.

Romans 12:1–2

THE GOOD LIFE
Romans 12:1–2

Pleasing to God
(comfortable in
God's presence)

Holy (comfortable
with self; not
falling short)

Renewed Mind
(understanding God's
thoughts: freedom from
uncertainty)

Living Sacrifice
(sense of goal,
purpose in life)

Doing God's will
(sense of
accomplishment)

VS. THE EMPTY LIFE

can't do things right

sense of shame or guilt

+sharing, stubborness, ungiving

less self confidence

less joy, satisfaction

anger

lack of self control

cold, w/o love or caring

no motivation to study scripture

doubt that God hears

time wasted, days not purposeful

uncomfortable ī God, self, others

uncertainty, fear, lack of
direction,

less responsive to others, isolated

too self critical, no self praise

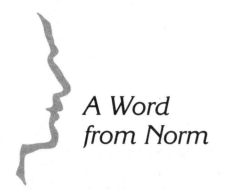

A Word from Norm

Have one person
read this brief
word from Norm
aloud. Then discuss
the questions at the end.

Ever play a word association game? You hear a word, and quickly say its opposite. Fat/thin. Short/tall. Black/white. Good/ ? You want to say "bad," don't you? Most do. But when we speak of the good life, a "bad" life is not really its opposite.

For the child of God, I believe that the opposite of the good life is an *empty life.* Why empty? Because if Jesus is not allowed to fill our lives with His goodness, what we experience *is* emptiness. The prophet Haggai spoke powerfully of this emptiness.

"Give careful thought to your ways. You have planted much, but have harvested little. You eat, but never have enough. You drink, but never have your fill. You put on clothes, but are not warm. You earn wages, only to put them in a purse with holes in it" (Hag. 1:5–7).

Empty! The people yearned for abundance, but apart from God. It is impossible for a people to prosper with that attitude.

Our loving Father wants to liberate us from emptiness in all its expressions. He wants to free us through goodness from a life empty of meaning. Many hurry about their daily activities and never pause to ask, "What is life all about?" Even Christians fail to discover meaning in life through their relationship with Jesus Christ. A busy life may keep mind and body occupied, but the emptiness is there.

Through goodness God wants to free us from a life empty of worthwhile goals. I may substitute activities that I hope will satisfy my inner hunger, but they never do. My achievements and successes are never as significant as I anticipated, and the emptiness is there.

Through goodness God wants to free us from a life empty of fulfillment. The empty feeling persists. I may have an abundance of material possessions, a secure job, and social status, but without God's kind of goodness fulfillment evades me.

Through goodness God wants to free us from a life empty of contentment. Without goodness life lacks peace and joy. Without goodness I have allowed the world system—its way of thinking—to squeeze me into a mold of selfishness, and to squeeze out the beauty of a truly worthwhile life.

The tragic routine of an empty life can be broken, and a good life can be established. Building God's kind of good life can establish a pattern that He intends to bring us the abundance Jesus promised for His people.

Discuss

1 Which characteristic of an "empty life" is most painful or destructive?

2 Which of the "by-products" of a good life is most important to you personally?

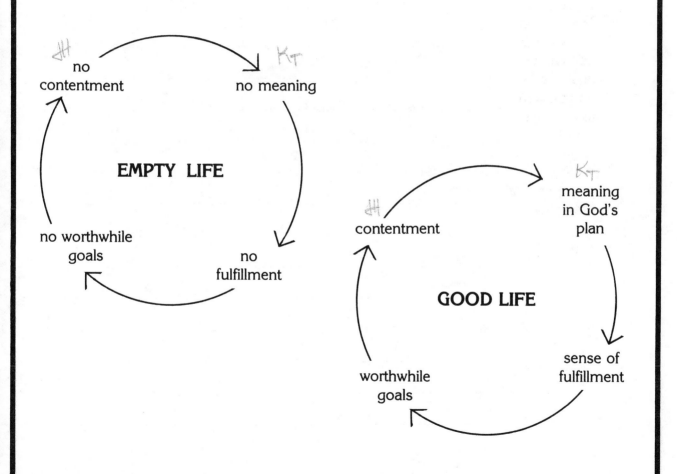

WRITE

Look ahead five years. What kind of person do you want to be? What qualities do you want to characterize your life?

Write out your personal projection here.

In five years,

open minded & accepting giving person, peaceful, ē joy & hope in my life. I want to be a symbol of simplicity, not yet trapped by worldly goods & values. I want to be a spiritual person, & know F part of myself more completely. Mostly I desire calmness & gentleness in my life, ē a sense of direction, & open acceptance to changes - that I might greet Δ ē energy & excitement. I hope to also maintain a playful, laughing heart. KT

In five years, I want to be helping to organize and run some part of a hunger project; To be able to see the joy in their faces and show F someone really cares. To Have others know me as a loving, caring person who would always lend a helping hand. To be able to help solve others problems and bring peace and happiness to their lives so they could do the same for others. To trust in God to help me. JH

12

STEPS
toward *your* good life.

This discipleship experience is designed to help you take practical steps toward the good life which God calls you to . . . with all its benefits. Here is how the discipleship process operates:

1 You'll gather weekly with the others in your group to share the process.

2 Together you'll discover what God's good life involves by exploring Romans 12 through 16.

3 You will choose a partner, who will be your special prayer focus and with whom you will have additional weekly times together.

4 You will keep a daily journal, in which you record your growth and application of God's Word . . . and in which you record what God is teaching you, through His children as well as through Scripture.

In this process you will encourage each other to follow Jesus daily. And you will grow in your ability to live His kind of truly good life.

CHOOSE A PARTNER

You and your partner will (1) pray for each other daily, and (2) meet or talk together on the phone at least once a week. You may want to meet for coffee, or breakfast or lunch. When you're together share what you've recorded in your journal. And share prayer requests. And, of course, make prayer together a part of your meetings.

Now select your partner and record the following information:

My partner's name _Snoopy , Goldie_

Partner's address _Home Orinda   Home Davis_

Partner's phone _Can't use phone w/o help_

Appointment time _to be scheduled @ session_

Appointment place _TBS_

SPEND

any final minutes with your partner and share which of these quotes (if any) most accurately reflects your past ideas of the good life.

If none, what was your idea of the good life five years ago?

"Each person's life is unique, separate from every other life. No one else can live your life, what you feel, get into your body and experience the world the way you do. It's the only life you get, and it's too precious to let others take advantage of it. Your functioning ought to bring you the joy of 'pulling your own strings.'"[1]

"Looking out for Number One is the conscious, rational effort to spend as much time as possible doing those things which will bring you the greatest amount of pleasure, and the less time on those which cause pain."[2]

"You deserve to be rich, and you can be rich. *Money-love* can help you have a life of abundance, filled with love and creativity and, incidentally, all the cash you want. It's as simple as this. Thinking rich will make you rich."[3]

---

[1]Wayne Dyer, *Pulling Your Own Strings* (New York: Avon, 1979).
[2]Robert J. Ringer, *Looking Out for Number One* (New York: Fawcett, 1978).
[3]Jerry Gillis, *Money-love* (New York: Warner Paperback Library).

JOURNAL

READ ROMANS 12:1–2 DAILY

DAY 1 Mon 2/10

It is late, I just finished typing up a portion of a lab due tomorrow. Talked w/ Amy and Sara tonight about going to church together on Wednesday. Amy's parents will be up and will hopefully join us.

DAY 2 Tue 2/11

DAY 3 Wed 2/12 [Ash-Wednesday]

Talked w/ a person who was in one of my classes last semester. He is trying to find enough time to get things together in time for doing missionary work in the 3rd world area. It is hard to find time to sit down relax and be w/ God alone, uninterrupted for more than a few minutes. I am constantly running, talking w/ God as I run from one place to another. My friend seemed to be able to take time, and I want to make it easier and more a part of my routine to spend more time w/ God.

DAY 4

DAY 5

DAY 6

LIFE TOGETHER  2

Romans 12:3–13

God's portrait
of His good life
for His people
begins with
an important realization.
He has called us
to live as brothers and sisters
in His new community.
We need to
understand ourselves
in relationship.

LET'S START WITH YOU

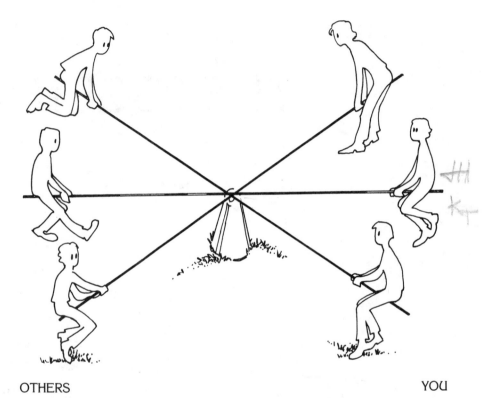

OTHERS   YOU

Think about yourself in relation to other Christians. Imagine you are on the *right side* of this teeter-totter. Where, in comparison with others, would you place yourself? Above? Below? On the same level? Color in with pen or pencil the teeter-totter that most closely represents where you feel you are in relation to other believers.

WHY?

What criteria did you use in evaluating yourself when you chose which teeter-totter to color in? Write down here the most important reasons (write up to three reasons) *why* you feel your choice represents you in relation to other Christians.

Note: You will *not* be asked to share these reasons.

1   ① openess of my relationship ī God - is my spirituality appearant to all who know me?

    ② Amt. of time spent in prayer/quiet time knowing God "Be still & know I am God" Ps...

2   ③ Christian Growth - time/energy devoted to a christian community - Bible study, also evangelism - sharing my faith,

    ① I feel on the low level for actual scripture knowledge and referencing. I have a good over view but still somewhat slight

3   ② My desire for active participation and life style, do feel is a little bit higher

    ③ I have a very high desire to become more active & more learned in my every day life style. of scripture

A Word
from Larry

For by the grace given me I say to every one of you: Do not think of yourself more highly than you ought, but rather think of yourself with sober judgment, in accordance with the measure of faith God has given you. Just as each of us has one body with many members, and these members do not all have the same function, so in Christ we who are many form one body, and each member belongs to all the others.

Romans 12:3–5

Study the Bible
passage and
commentary
individually
for eight minutes.

Underline any
thoughts which
seem particularly
significant, or which
help you understand
where on that
teeter-totter
God sees you.

Both the *up* and *down* teeter-totter positions are inaccurate pictures of who you and I are in relation to other believers. Our understanding of ourselves begins with the realization that in Christ we and others are equally contributing members of one Body. We each belong to the others. We each, while we do have different functions, are necessary to complete the whole.

From God's point of view, the equal teeter-totter represents who you and I are in relation to others. Each of us, in our different way, is equally necessary to the other.

When it comes to living God's good life, we need to understand that the good life is a life lived *together,* and that in our "together" relationship in the Body we are equally important.

We have different gifts, according to the grace given us. If a man's gift is prophesying, let him use it in proportion to his faith. If it is serving, let him serve; if it is teaching, let him teach; if it is encouraging, let him encourage; if it is contributing to the needs of others, let him give generously; if it is leadership, let him govern diligently; if it is showing mercy, let him do it cheerfully.

Romans 12:6–8

To say that you and I are equally important in the Body of Christ is not to suggest that we are the same. Our equality and our importance are related to a wonderful reality. God has given you, me, and every other believer a *gift* . . . a special way in which we can contribute to the well-being of others.

This fact gives us great insight into the nature of God's good life. The good life involves *using* whatever abilities God has given us to serve our brothers and sisters. There are many ways we can serve. While different, each way is necessary to the well-being of our brothers and sisters, and thus all are equally necessary.

If my gift is speaking out boldly to express God's viewpoint, I'm to do so. If it's serving others, I'm to serve. If it is helping my brother or sister grasp how God's Word can be applied in his or her life, I'm to teach. Whatever my way of contributing, I am to actively, diligently, and cheerfully serve. This is how our good life begins in the Body.

Love must be sincere. Hate what is evil; cling to what is good. Be devoted to one another in brotherly love. Honor one another above yourselves. Never be lacking in zeal, but keep your spiritual fervor, serving the Lord. Be joyful in hope, patient in affliction, faithful in prayer. Share with God's people who are in need. Practice hospitality.

Romans 12:9–13

If we are to truly serve each other as God's people, we must learn to live together in mutual love and respect. So the good life means building loving relationships with others in the Body.

What helps us to keep that teeter-totter in balance is to view one another from God's perspective . . . to see each one as important, as gifted, and as worthy of love and honor. And to realize that our brothers and sisters see us the same way. When we reject the world's criteria for evaluating ourselves and others, and use the criteria established by God, we are freed to love sincerely, and to serve cheerfully.

TOGETHER

as a group select *one* of the gifts from
Romans 12:5–9 to write in the circle.
Then discuss how the presence or ab-
sence of the qualities of Romans
12:9–13 would affect effectiveness in
serving others with this gift.

If there is time, do the same analysis
with another gift.

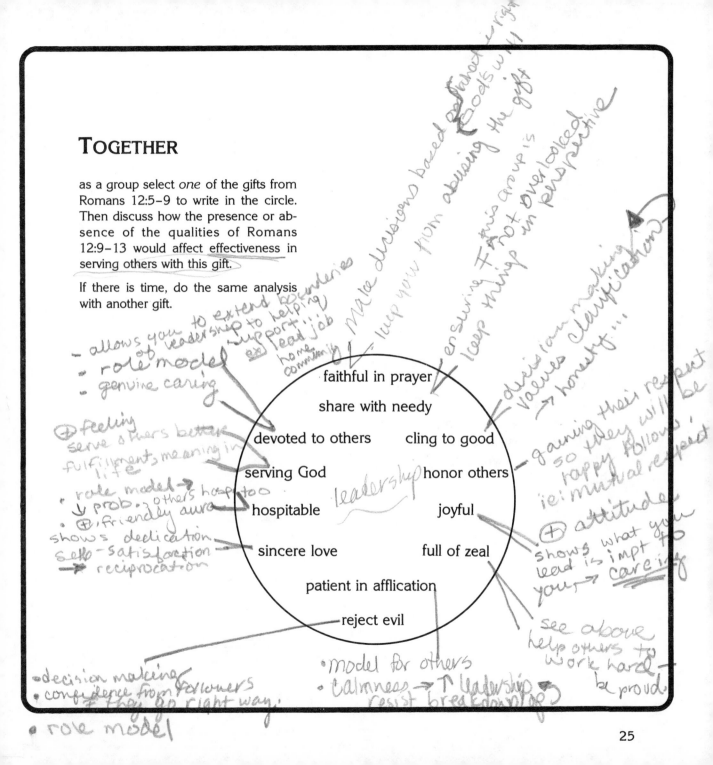

faithful in prayer

share with needy

devoted to others   cling to good

serving God   honor others

leadership

hospitable   joyful

sincere love   full of zeal

patient in afflication

reject evil

Handwritten annotations:

- allows you to extend boundaries of leadership to helping support
- role model
- genuine caring

ex: lead job
home community

make decisions based on shared organization/God's will
keep you from abusing the gift

ensuring # this group is not overlooked
keep things in perspective

decision making clarification
values
→ honesty...

⊕ feeling
serve others better
fulfillment, meaning in life

· role model → others hosp too
↓ prob.
· ⊕ friendly aura
shows dedication
self-satisfaction
→ reciprocation

gaining their respect
so they will be
happy followers
ie: mutual respect

⊕ attitudes
shows what you lead is impt to
you → caring

see above
help others to
work hard
be proud

· decision making
· confidence from followers
→ they go right way.

· model for others
· calmness → ↑ leadership
resist breakdown

· role model

LIST

individuals you know
who are
the kind of persons
described in
12:9–13.

J H
SYT/DT   sheryl, Dan
Fr. Pat / Bob   John
KT   Amy, Sara
Barbra in S.J.   Fr. Bob
Amy Sara Kathy   Laura / anne
                                Katie
                                H. Family
                                Cheryl + Family

WRITE

In what ways do you
see each of the individuals
you listed ministering to
others? Write down your
insights.

_____

_____

_____

_____

_____

CONCLUSION

Talk together about
each of these summary
statements and complete
the thoughts.

1 The good life God calls me to is one of service to my brothers
and sisters in the Body, so I _Can show them some of the good_
life ← I know

~ will serve

2 Living the good life as God has designed it means building a
relationship of love with others, so I _can teach love, teach God_

~ will love
~ will support, care ↔ help others

3 In God's plan I am truly important in relation to other Christians
because _we are all bound together, as common_
"members of the body of christ."

Use your final minutes together to pray that God will help
each of you grow into more loving, more effectively
ministering, disciples of Jesus Christ.

JOURNAL

READ 1 CORINTHIANS 13 DAILY

DAY 1

DAY 2

DAY 3

DAY 4

DAY 5

DAY 6

Look back at pages 20 and 21. What changes would you make now in what you wrote?

OVERCOMING EVIL WITH GOOD 3

Romans 12:14–21

Each of us
has some relationship
with a person or persons
who could be called "difficult."
God's calling
to the good life
shows us how to deal with
difficult relationships,
and by doing good
overcome the evil
that might result.

WRITE

a brief letter
to "Dear Abby"
describing
one difficult person
you have to
deal with.

_____

_____

_____

_____

_____

_____

_____

_____

_____

_____

_____

_____

_____

CIRCLE

On the right are a number of words used or implied in Romans 12:14–21. Circle any of them which characterize the difficult person you described in your "Dear Abby" letter.

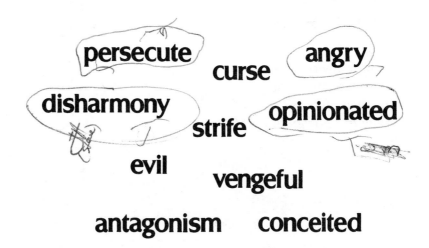

persecute   curse   angry

disharmony   strife   opinionated

evil   vengeful

antagonism   conceited

Bless those who persecute you; bless and do not curse. Rejoice with those who rejoice; mourn with those who mourn. Live in harmony with one another. Do not be proud, but be willing to associate with people of low position. Do not be conceited.

Do not repay anyone evil for evil. Be careful to do what is right in the eyes of everybody. If it is possible, as far as it depends on you, live at peace with everyone. Do not take revenge, my friends, but leave room for God's wrath, for it is written: "It is mine to avenge; I will repay," says the Lord. On the contrary:

"If your enemy is hungry, feed him; if he is thirsty, give him something to drink. In doing this, you will heap burning coals on his head."

Do not be overcome by evil, but overcome evil with good.

Romans 12:14–21

COMPARE
WITH OTHERS

How many of you
circled each of the
following words?
Tally the numbers here.

⊥	persecute	___	curse
2	disharmony	___	evil
⊥	opinionated	___	strife
⊥	angry	___	vengeful
___	antagonism	___	conceit

SHARE

Why has it been hard
to break the pattern
of the relationship?
Take
just a few
minutes
to compare.

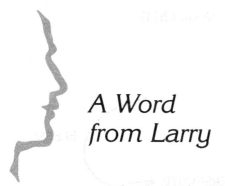

A Word from Larry

Have one person
read aloud
as background
for the next
activity.

Psychologists have a term for what Paul deals with in Romans 12:14–21. It's called the "norm of reciprocity." Its meaning is simple. We tend to treat people as they treat us.

Someone invites us over for dinner. We're likely to invite them. Someone smiles when we meet them. We smile in return. Or, someone barks angrily . . . and before we're aware of it our voice is brusque and angry too.

In difficult relationships it's common for this kind of reaction to others to build up over time, until a tragic pattern has been established. Dislike or strife or anger have been reinforced over and over again. Now the programmed emotions take control, with anger feeding anger, evil on evil. No wonder Paul warns us "do not be overcome by evil!"

But Paul goes on. "Overcome evil with good." God's call to the good life gives us guidance for overcoming the evil in our most difficult relationships by substituting the *good* response for the normal response of reciprocity to another's attack. When we respond with good rather than match the evil we are, in the words of Paul, "overcoming evil with good."

On the next page you'll look at some of the negative patterns that develop in difficult relationships. And you'll go on to look at Romans 12:14–21 again to see how God tells us to overcome such evil with His good.

THE CYCLE

"Bless those who persecute you; bless and do not curse" (Rom. 12:14).

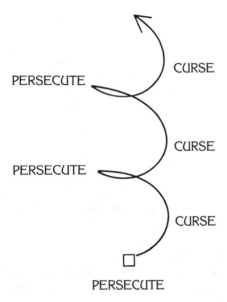

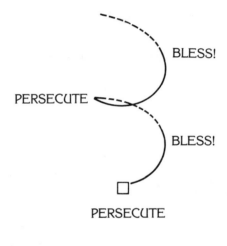

The normal pattern of reciprocity is shown in Romans 12:14. Persecution is reacted to with anger and cursing. The cycle continues, and the antagonism grows.

God's good life way is to break the self-reinforcing cycle. Evil *can* be overcome . . . even in others . . . by good. We are to do all we can to keep a "difficult relationship" from growing by substituting a good response to evil, rather than to react normally "in kind."

WORK TOGETHER

to discover the *good* that breaks the patterns
shown in Romans 12. Fill in this chart.

	EVIL ACT	NORMAL RESPONSE	GOOD RESPONSE
v. 14	*persecute*	*curse*	*bless*
v. 16b	*CONCEIT*	*″*	*″*
v. 17	*EVIL*	*persecute*	*accept & excuse*
v. 19	*Vengeful*	*defend/anger*	*ignore*
v. 20			
other			
other			

Bless those who persecute you; bless and do not curse. Rejoice with those who rejoice; mourn with those who mourn. Live in harmony with one another. Do not be proud, but be willing to associate with people of low position. Do not be conceited.

Do not repay anyone evil for evil. Be careful to do what is right in the eyes of everybody. If it is possible, as far as it depends on you, live at peace with everyone. Do not take revenge, my friends, but leave room for God's wrath, for it is written: "It is mine to avenge; I will repay," says the Lord. On the contrary:

"If your enemy is hungry, feed him; if he is thirsty, give him something to drink. In doing this, you will heap burning coals on his head."

Do not be overcome by evil, but overcome evil with good.

Romans 12:14–21

SHARE

In groups of four
share your "Dear Abby" letters.
Together analyze
the action/reaction pattern
in each,
and suggest ways
to overcome
any evils with good.

PERSON	EVIL	NORMAL REACTION	GOOD OVERCOMING ACTION
Tommy	Condescending remarks.	quick comeback	ignore
	Stupid rules	Refuse / fight	ignore / forget / discuss
	demands attention	ignore	equal attention
Steve	disharmony due to lack of self confidence	avoid	include him & give support

THIS WEEK

Pray for the others in your foursome.

Keep a record in your journal of your daily relationships with the difficult person you identified on page 32.

Meditate daily on Joseph's life as an example of one who also had difficult relationships yet overcame through good. Record your insights and share them with your partner this week.

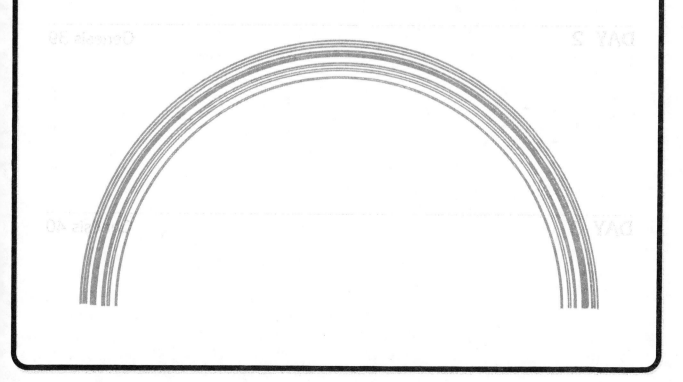

JOURNAL

DAY 1 Genesis 37

DAY 2 Genesis 39

DAY 3 Genesis 40

Genesis 41   **DAY 4**

Genesis 45   **DAY 5**

Genesis 50   **DAY 6**

ENCOURAGEMENT 4

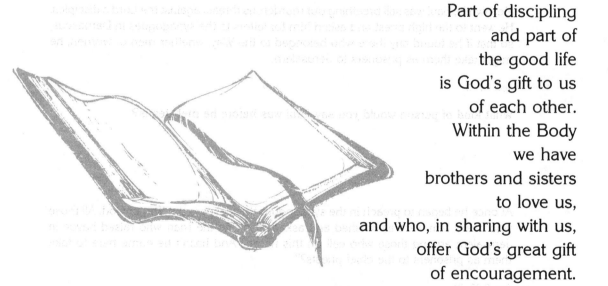

Part of discipling
and part of
the good life
is God's gift to us
of each other.
Within the Body
we have
brothers and sisters
to love us,
and who, in sharing with us,
offer God's great gift
of encouragement.

A CASE HISTORY
of encouragement

Imagine yourselves to be members of the early church. Read and talk together about each question.

who WAS the high priest?? WAS he a STATe leader too?

Meanwhile, Saul was still breathing out murderous threats against the Lord's disciples. He went to the high priest and asked him for letters to the synagogues in Damascus, so that if he found any there who belonged to the Way, whether men or women, he might take them as prisoners to Jerusalem.

Acts 9:1–2

What kind of person would you say Paul was before he met Jesus?

He seemed to be very misguided. Saw Jesus as as a threat to his way of life, religion, etc.

At once he began to preach in the synagogues that Jesus is the Son of God. All those who heard him were astonished and asked, "Isn't he the man who raised havoc in Jerusalem among those who call on this name? And hasn't he come here to take them as prisoners to the chief priests?"

Acts 9:20–21

How do you think the report of Paul's transformation affected believers who heard of it? *A powerful effect having someone so strongly against Jesus all of a sudden turn around and publicly praise him.*

44

When he came to Jerusalem, he tried to join the disciples, but they were all afraid of him, not believing that he really was a disciple. But Barnabas took him and brought him to the apostles. He told them how Saul on his journey had seen the Lord and that the Lord had spoken to him, and how in Damascus he had preached fearlessly in the name of Jesus.

Acts 9:26–27

What encouragement did Barnabas help the church experience by listening to Paul . . . and sharing his story with the whole Body?

gave validity + strength to Paul's story

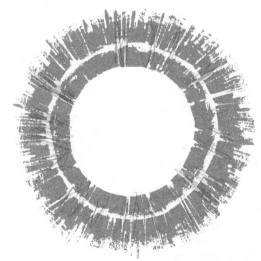

ENCOURAGEMENT
One way God encourages us is by sharing with each other what He has done in our lives.

A Word
from Norm

Take a few minutes
to read this
brief report from Norm.

Looking back, I see many ways that God has been at work in my life. His presence and His ministry of love to me has led me step by step into greater experiences of the good life.

I began life completely ignorant of God. Until I was twelve years old my knowledge of Him consisted mainly of superstition and folklore. "When it thunders God is bowling in heaven" is the kind of thing my friends and I used to believe. Then God used an elderly lady in a candy store and a sensitive Sunday school teacher to introduce me to God's love. And I stepped into a life-changing relationship with Jesus Christ.

In those early years I struggled with feelings of inferiority. I was shy and felt very inadequate. I actually disliked myself. No one in my family had any education beyond high school, and I was sure that I would be unable to achieve anything significant. But God began a rebuilding process. The indwelling Spirit affirmed my worth and value. Christian friends encouraged me. The Word of God strengthened me. And I found a new perspective on myself. I began to see that Christ's love documented my worth to Him, and His strength made me sufficient.

One consequence of those early feelings of inferiority was loneliness. I backed away from relationships with people, fearing that they would discover my incompetence. I was easily embarrassed in groups, feeling awkward and conspicuous. I was a loner, not because I enjoyed it, but because I feared others.

But God was good to me. Patiently, He won my friendship. I found Christian friends, who drew me by their love. I met the girl who would later become my wife, and she helped me relate in a deeper way to another individual. Most recently, a fellowship of Christians has provided a new dimension of belonging. And I've left behind my loneliness.

There are many other blessings God has given me as I've learned to live His good life. I'm indebted to Him for what He's taught me about legalism. How delightful it is to be freed from negative thoughts, and enslavement to "do's" and "don'ts" which used to fill my life with false guilt or false pride.

It's good to look back and see all that God has done in my life. It gives me great confidence that God will continue to do His transforming work in me. And it lifts my heart in praise.

SHARE
for about
five minutes.
How does God's
work in Norm
encourage you?

WHAT
has God been
doing in *your* life?

The stairs represent progress
toward your own transformation and
experience of the good life. Draw a
stick figure in to represent where
you are on the stairway.

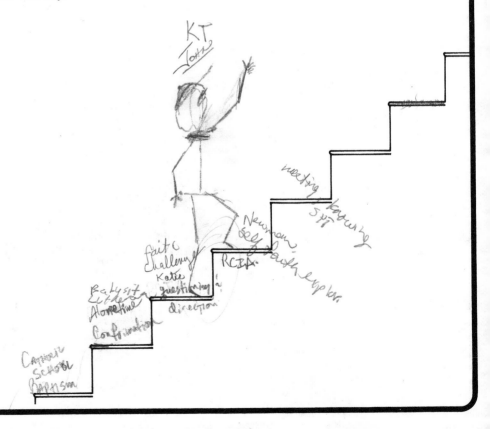

THE GOAL OF THE GOOD LIFE

Look back over your life as a Christian. What has God done in your life? On each of the steps below the one where you drew your stick figure, jot down one way in which God has worked His good in you.

SHARE

in groups of
six.

Share what you've written on each step with the others in
your small group. Encourage each other with your report
of God's work in your life. Then pray, and thank God for
His working . . . and encouragement.

THIS WEEK
Read Psalm 147
daily and praise
God for His
working in you.

JOURNAL

DAY 1

DAY 2

DAY 3

DAY 4

DAY 5

DAY 6

DOWN UNDER 5

Romans 13:1–7

Everyone who lives
in human society
lives "under"
institutions and authorities.
This isn't always easy,
especially if
the institutions are unjust
or the authorities unfair.
But learning how
to live "down under"
is important to
the truly good life.

KSRL
Television Israel
interviews David the King

KSRL: David, tell us about your early days with Saul.

DAVID: After the Lord helped me destroy Goliath, Saul insisted I remain with him. As I advanced in the army, the people began to compare my exploits with Saul's. Eventually Saul became angry and jealous, and tried to kill me (*see* 1 Sam. 18:1–11).

KSRL: Those were difficult times. Why didn't you rebel and seize the throne as Saul feared?

DAVID: I couldn't rebel against a man God had placed in authority.

KSRL: Even though he unjustly threatened your life?

DAVID: He did that. Once I told Jonathan, "There is only a step between me and death." But the two times I could have killed Saul, when my close friends urged me to do it and even said God wanted me to kill him for "God has delivered him into your hands," I refused.

KSRL: You felt very deeply that you should not rebel?

DAVID: Yes. I even felt deep conviction when I cut off only the corner of Saul's robe, to prove to him that I could have killed him (*see* 1 Sam. 24:1–5).

KSRL: Why?

DAVID: I told my men the reason. "God forbid," I said, "that I should do evil against my master, the LORD's anointed" (*see* 1 Sam. 24:6–7).

KSRL: You recognized Saul as your master even after he tried to kill you?

DAVID: Saul was God's appointed leader for Israel at that time. I honored him as such. I was confident all along that the Lord is sovereign. He could do what He chose with Saul. I did not need to take matters into my own hands (*see* 1 Sam. 26:10).

Discuss

1 Look back over the David interview. Discuss how David's responses to authority were godly.

2 Analyze the Scripture passage on the next page. What principles of godly response can you see in this passage? Begin by reading the passage privately. *Underline* each thought that suggests a *principle.*

Everyone must submit himself to the governing authorities, for there is no authority except that which God has established. The authorities that exist have been established by God. Consequently, he who rebels against the authority is rebelling against what God has instituted, and those who do so will bring judgment on themselves. For rulers hold no terror for those who do right, but for those who do wrong. Do you want to be free from fear of the one in authority? Then do what is right and he will commend you. For he is God's servant to do you good. But if you do wrong, be afraid, for he does not bear the sword for nothing. He is God's servant, an agent of wrath to bring punishment on the wrongdoer. Therefore, it is necessary to submit to the authorities, not only because of possible punishment but also because of conscience.

This is also why you pay taxes, for the authorities are God's servants, who give their full time to governing. Give everyone what you owe him: If you owe taxes, pay taxes; if revenue, then revenue; if respect, then respect; if honor, then honor.

Romans 13:1–7

TOGETHER

Agree on
clear statements
of principles
which would guide
you to respond to
authorities and institutions
in a godly way.

_____

_____

_____

_____

_____

_____

_____

_____

_____

_____

_____

_____

PRESSURE

Here are
some of the pressures
that were on David,
which might have led him
to violate godly principles
of response to
authority.

David was aware
he was to replace
Saul

A natural reaction
against unfairness

Pressure from
friends

A desire for
revenge (anger)

Saul was acting
against God's will

Saul's unfairness

Personal losses
(financial, position,
etc.)

DISCUSS

What similar
or additional pressures
exist today?
Think of
a person or authority
with which you experience tension,
and list together
sources of pressure
which make it difficult
to respond
in a godly way.

2000 LBS

THE GOOD LIFE

involves choosing to live "under" authorities and institutions in the godly way defined by Romans 13 and demonstrated by David.

Close your time together by reviewing the principles you defined (p. 57), and praying that each might find grace to live by them rather than submit to pressures.

THIS WEEK
Meditate on
the experiences
from David's life
found in 1 Samuel 24.
Share your insights
with your partner.

A Word from Norm

*A personal meditation
for this coming week*

Seeing life from God's perspective can be revolutionary . . . and life changing. We discover a way of living that liberates us from frustration, anxiety and defeat. As we experientially know the truth, we enjoy the freedom it brings (John 8:32).

God has told us how we are to relate to authorities and institutions He has ordained. We can be confident that what He has designed will be for our good . . . if we respond with humility and obedience. Cooperating with God's life principles leads us to enjoy the benefits of this blessing.

Submitting to those appointed to lead us frees us from feelings of guilt. David was sensitive to God's appointment of Saul as king. The simple act of cutting off a corner of his robe bothered David's conscience (1 Sam. 24:5). Perhaps he sensed that he was expressing a spirit of defiance in that act.

When I was a young man I sometimes drove my automobile in excess of the speed limit. It caused me to feel uneasy, even frightened, if I saw a police car. I would feel this way even when I drove at the speed limit. I feared God-appointed authority. As I have matured I realize that speed limits are established for the safety of mankind. I choose to obey them. My fear of police cars has vanished.

Submitting to authority gives us the joy and peace of knowing that we are doing right. Paul wrote to the Galatians, "A man reaps what he sows" (Gal. 6:7). Sowing the seeds of humility gives a harvest of inner peace. I experience the joy of knowing that I am honoring my heavenly Father, not sowing rebellion and disorder.

Submitting to God-appointed authorities and institutions benefits me in another way: the authority is not against me. The authority does not become suspicious of my conduct, constantly watching me to see what trouble I will generate. Rather, those leaders will see me as cooperating with them, seeking to live in harmony with their directives. I will gain their respect. They will learn that I am trustworthy and eager to support them in a function they are called to fulfill. The dependable, cooperative employee is more likely to gain the respect and benefits from his employer; the harmonious student gains the teacher's support and favor.

In essence, the Christian who whole-heartedly submits to authorities and institutions enjoys the fruit of the good life. This applies in all areas of life—family, school, work, church, government. Men and women who exhibit the spirit of Joseph, Daniel and Paul are not threatened when asked to submit to ruling authorities. As a result they enjoy inner peace, and frequently are honored with responsible positions by those who observe their holy behavior.

Journal

DAY 1

DAY 2

DAY 3

DAY 4

DAY 5

DAY 6

OUTREACH 6

Romans 13:8–14

In living the good life
we live among persons
who are not yet Christians.
How do we
relate to them?
Many people
offer their ideas—
from withdrawal
to aggressive witnessing—
about what the answer
should be.
Romans gives us
a very helpful perspective.

ON YOUR OWN
Circle the three *best*
approaches to evangelism.
Cross out the three worst.

give a tract

get kids in for cookies
and use flannelgraph

join their club

invite to church
evangelistic meetings

have a home Bible study

help neighbor on
work project

go to cocktail party
at a neighbor's

open windows and turn
radio evangelist up loud

take neighbor fishing

bake cake and ice
it with John 3:16

use the four
spiritual laws

invite to an
evangelical movie

loan or give
books

put "please don't
smoke, I'm a born-
again Christian"
signs around the house

say open grace
in restuarants

invite your pastor
to a neighborhood
party

join a "great books"
club

put on evangelistic
bumper sticker

employ
non-Christians

put Bible verses
on billboards

have friends
in for dinner

house to house
visitation

street meetings

friendship dinners
at restaurants
with special speakers

carry sandwich
board sign: repent

write lettters to
the editor

call a radio
call-in program

DISCUSS

In groups
of four
compare the items circled
and those crossed out.

1 Why did each of you choose the approaches you circled?

2 Why did you choose the ones you crossed out?

SHARE

What actions by a Christian(s) were instrumental in *your* conversion? Share two or three things each. Jot down notes on each person's experiences.

1 _____

_____

_____

2 _____

_____

_____

3 _____

_____

_____

4 _____

_____

_____

A Word from Larry

Bible Background on Romans 13:8–14

This Romans passage is not *directly* about evangelism. It is instead about the way God's good life is expressed in our relationships with our neighbors. It helps us to see and understand the *relational context* in which those who do not yet know Christ are influenced to consider and to respond to the gospel.

The key to our relationship with those who are our neighbors (13:9–10) is love. As we actively love our neighbors we fulfill "the continuing debt to love . . . our fellow man" (13:8) and completely fulfill the Law.

On the next page you'll look together at the commandments Paul refers to in this passage, and see how breaking each denies our neighbor love. And how actively reaching out in love does fulfill the commandments.

Look over the chart in your groups of four, and see if you can relate *active loving* to the actions of individuals you described as instrumental in your own coming to Christ.

LOVE YOUR NEIGHBOR

Let no debt remain outstanding, except the continuing debt to love one another, for he who loves his fellow man has fulfilled the law. The commandments, "Do not commit adultery," "Do not murder," "Do not steal," "Do not covet," and whatever other commandment there may be, are summed up in this one rule: "Love your neighbor as yourself." Love does no harm to its neighbor. Therefore love is the fulfillment of the law.

Romans 13:8–10

LAW	PRACTICAL IMPLICATIONS (not loving)	POSITIVE OPPOSITES (loving)
do not commit adultery	impure relationship, use of others for personal pleasure	pure relationship, care about others for their sake, serve not use others
do not murder	tears down, takes away from, or deminishes another as a person, kills worth and value	enhances and adds to anothers person and sense of personal worth and value as shaped in God's image
do not steal	take away money, reputation, job, undermine relationships [anything of value]	give, to add value to their life. Build reputation, help train for better job, etc.
do not covet	attitude of envy, grudge others what they have, show discontent	show good things received from God, contentment with His gifts. Have positive attitude, values which others will pick up

UNDERLINE
Together underline
phrases that
indicate we are
to be aggressively
involved in
loving.

And do this, understanding the present time. The hour has
come for you to wake up from your slumber, because our
salvation is nearer now than when we first believed. The night is
nearly over; the day is almost here. So let us put aside the
deeds of darkness and put on the armor of light. Let us behave
decently, as in the daytime, not in orgies and drunkenness, not
in sexual immorality and debauchery, not in dissension and
jealousy. Rather, clothe yourselves with the Lord Jesus Christ,
and do not think about how to gratify the desires of the sinful
nature.

Romans 13:11–14

The good life is ACTIVE involvement in loving.

Pursue
the good life.

Right now with your partner, discuss how *you* can put love for your neighbor into practice this week. And pray with each other that God will make this aspect of His good life more and more a part of yours.

This week

Meditate on John 3:9 daily.

Be sure to meet with or call your partner.

Journal

_____
                                         DAY 1

_____
                                         DAY 2

_____
                                         DAY 3

DAY 4

DAY 5

DAY 6

MY DO'S, YOUR DON'TS 7

Romans 14:1–9

Christians have
different convictions.
Sometimes
it's difficult to know
how to relate
to a person
whose convictions
differ from ours.
How should we
feel about them?
What should
we do?

A Word from Norm

Read individually
and then write your answers.

We've all been taught that there are certain things that are right and others that are wrong. We've been told, for instance, that "As a parent, you ought to. . . ." And we've all been told that "As a Christian, you ought to. . . ."

There are two things important to think about when we explore "ought to's." One is the *source* of the supposed obligation. And the second is how we can *communicate* convictions fairly and effectively. Let's look at each issue.

The source. We can see four. One is that of biblical statement. "Share with God's people in need" as well as "do not murder" are statements about the kind of life which is appropriate for God's children.

But many of our ideas about what we ought to do come from other sources. Another source is *personal conviction.* I distinguish personal convictions from the first category in this simple way: Biblical statements are statements made in Scripture. Personal convictions are based on my *interpretation* of Scripture. For instance, what about the role of women in the church? Or remarriage after divorce?

A third source is *personal preferences.* Usually these have a cultural rather than biblical basis. For instance, most Americans prefer to have church services at 11 A.M. Sunday morning. We may get very emotional about such a practice being right, but we can't say it is derived from a biblical statement or interpretation.

And then of course there is the fourth source of "ought to's." Personal *hang-ups.* These are my own peculiarities or idiosyncrasies. Don't chew gum with your mouth open. Don't wear jeans (or pants suits) to church.

So when we begin to think about the area of "ought to's" and our relationship with others, it's good to distinguish the sources of those things which we feel are right or wrong.

Communicating effectively. Usually the more strongly we feel about "ought to's" the less effective we are in communicating them. Particularly if we act and evaluate in a role rather than in a relationship. By acting or thinking in a role I mean making a judgment about an action on the basis of its rightness or wrongness *because of the role you have.* "You are a parent, so you *must.* . . ." We do not relate to the person as an individual, but in his or her role as a parent. And, "You are a Christian now, so you must. . . ." Here, too, our attitude is determined by our idea of what is appropriate to the role, not by our relationship with the individual. When we come at convictions from the "role" basis we tend to *demand* or *impose* behaviors. When we operate out of a relationship, we use different (and more effective) means to communicate. The chart below shows some of the differences.

The Romans passage we're about to study does not deal with the *source* of differences in "ought to" convictions. But it does deal with the *relationship with others* which we are to maintain in spite of differences.

Fill in the blanks

If we view others in a role, we feel we should _____ or _____ their convictions. If we operate from a relationship we will be more likely to

_____

_____

_____

SOURCE OF CONVICTION	TYPE OF COMMUNICATION	
	ROLE	RELATIONAL
biblical statement	demand	teach, discuss, appeal
personal convictions	impose	share reasons, encourage to consider
personal preferences	impose	share reasons, give freedom of individual choice
personal hang-ups	impose	confess as personal preference

Four sources of "ought to's" are . . .

1 _____   3 _____

2 _____   4 _____

TOGETHER

Spend five minutes
or so
sorting the following practices
into the four categories
and adding any other illustrations
you can think of.

attending Wednesday prayer meeting
not reading Sunday paper till Monday
handing out tracts to non-Christians
praying before meals
conducting daily family devotions
not listening to rock music

BIBLE STATEMENTS

_____

_____

_____

_____

CONVICTIONS

_____

_____

_____

_____

PREFERENCES

_____

_____

_____

_____

HANG-UPS

_____

_____

_____

_____

AN AFFIRMATION

We believe that areas of Christian freedom involve all issues beyond those of clear and specific biblical statement.

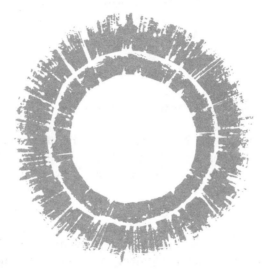

A QUESTION

How are we to relate to those whose freedom leads them to different convictions than our own on these other issues?

STUDY TOGETHER

The Passage

Accept him whose faith is weak, without passing judgment on disputable matters. One man's faith allows him to eat everything, but another man, whose faith is weak, eats only vegetables.

Romans 14:1–2

The Commentary *by Larry*

The word *accept* is an active rather than a passive one. God's instructions are that we *welcome* others, and that our welcome be generous and full—even though they and we may differ on "disputable matters."

One illustration of such a "disputable matter," which falls in the category of *conviction,* is whether or not a believer ought to eat meat or only vegetables. Each one makes his choice out of faith; we are not to pass judgment on others in such matters.

Discuss
The Question

In this passage, whose faith is weak? The one who says "Don't"—or the one who does?

The Passage

The man who eats everything must not look down on him who does not, and the man who does not eat everything must not condemn the man who does, for God has accepted him. Who are you to judge someone else's servant? To his own master he stands or falls. And he will stand, for the Lord is able to make him stand.

Romans 14:3–4

The Commentary *by Larry*

Typically differences that flow from deeply held personal convictions cause one of two reactions. The person who uses his freedom to "do" what the other will not do may ridicule or look down on the one who feels he cannot. And the one whose convictions say, "I do not" is all too likely to condemn the believer who does.

Paul says both these actions involve *judging;* in essence ruling on the "acceptability" of a brother or sister. But God has accepted our brother or sister into His Family! If God has accepted him or her on the basis of faith in Christ, how can we even suggest that he is not acceptable to us?

The final statement removes great pressure from us. We can share our convictions with others. But God has not called us to judge others. He alone is judge, for He alone is over our fellow servants and us. And God is able to make us . . . and those whose convictions differ . . . stand before Him.

The Question

What is the impact on personal relationships when another person condemns you, or looks down on you?

The Passage

One man considers one day more sacred than another; another man considers every day alike. Each one should be fully convinced in his own mind. He who regards one day as special, does so to the Lord. He who eats meat, eats to the Lord, for he gives thanks to God; and he who abstains, does so to the Lord and gives thanks to God. For none of us lives to himself alone and none of us dies to himself alone. If we live, we live to the Lord; and if we die, we die to the Lord. So, whether we live or die, we belong to the Lord.   *Romans 8:5–8*

The Commentary *by Larry*

Paul now gives another illustration of the kind of differences over convictions that disturb and divide the fellowship. Some focus on a single day of the week as sacred. Others see each day as alike. Some eat meat. Some do not. And of course we could each go on and add many other items to this sort of list.

But what is important, Paul says, is the *attitude toward God* with which we live out our convictions. "Each one should be fully convinced in his own mind," Paul stresses. And our conviction is essentially this: that what we are doing pleases the one who is our Lord in both life and death.

The impact of this teaching is striking. The man who eats meat (who "does"), convinced of his freedom and expressing thanks to God, has made the *right* choice! And the man who will not eat meat (who "doesn't"), out of a desire to please God, has also made the *right* choice! In each case it is the motivation, and the willingness of the individual to respond to Jesus as Lord, which makes the choice right or wrong. It is not the thing itself which is at issue.

The Question

How do we talk with another person whose convictions differ with ours, or whose practices are different, to let him know that it is the relationship we each have with Jesus that is important to us, and not the practice itself?

The Passage

For this very reason, Christ died and returned to life so that he might
be Lord of both the dead and the living.   *Romans 8:9*

The Commentary *by Larry*

This final statement is a powerful expression of Jesus' sole right to
Lordship over the Church.

Jesus Christ is not dead, nor is He "head emeritus," nor is He a
retired "chairman of the board." He has not placed into human
hands His right to lead, guide, control, and judge His people. No,
Jesus is risen, and His return to life was "so that he might be the
Lord both of the dead and the living."

To judge, or condemn, or to look down on others for their differing
convictions, is to deny Jesus the right to His Lordship and to attempt
to claim the right of control of another person who is His, not ours, to
control.

The Question

Have you ever felt others have demanded the right to direct your life,
your choices, and your actions? How did this affect your personal
relationship with Jesus?

After sharing, pray together, commiting yourselves to let Jesus be
Lord in the lives of other believers in your fellowship.

JOURNAL

READ ROMANS 14:1–9 DAILY

DAY 1

DAY 2

DAY 3

DAY 4

DAY 5

DAY 6

85

EVALUATE! 8

Romans 14:10–23

If in "doubtful things"
we are to welcome
and not judge
our brothers and sisters,
does it mean that
we are not
to evaluate?
That we simply
give up trying
to distinguish between
that which is
helpful or harmful,
good or bad?
Not at all!

CHECK
The conscience of the Christian community

In every culture and society, a "conscience of the Christian community" does develop. That is, certain things are felt by the community to be "wrong" for Christians. Thinking of the Christian community of which you are a part, which of the following are generally judged to be wrong or at least questionable? Place a check mark by those you believe are against the conscience of your community.

___ social drinking
___ playing cards
___ belonging to unions
___ smoking cigarettes
___ smoking pot
___ going to school dances
___ capital punishment
___ remarriage
___ driving an expensive car
___ witnessing in bars
___ using credit cards
___ eating meat
___ sports on Sunday
___ abortion
___ birth control
___ serving in the military

___ being in politics
___ not tithing
___ gambling
___ friendships with non-Christians
___ attending a secular rather than a Christian school
___ going to movies
___ watching TV
___ being a high school cheerleader
___ making a business profit
___ not attending midweek services

A Word from Larry

*Bible background on
Romans 14:10–23*

**Read individually
and underline key
points.**

Paul's argument (line of thought) in exploring the issue of the conscience of the community is very important to understand. Let's trace it, and then look together at Romans 14:10–23.

He begins by insisting that we are not to judge or to look down on our brothers. Believers will account for their choices to God. We are not to demand that others give account to us!

Instead of evaluating and judging others, Paul tells us to look, each one, at *ourselves!* We are not to evaluate *their* choices, but we *are* to evaluate our own.

But what criterion do we use to evaluate? Put simply, we are to evaluate the impact of our choices on the others in our fellowship, to be sure that nothing we do is an obstacle to their growth, or something that might lead them to an action which violates their conscience.

But what about the action itself? Aren't we to judge the rightness or wrongness of that? Here is Scripture's surprising announcement. "I am persuaded in the Lord Jesus that nothing is unclean in itself; but it is unclean for anyone who thinks it is unclean" (14:14 RSV). Any action against our conscience is wrong for us. Others are not.

But there is one more thing to consider! Even something which I have the freedom to do "as unto the Lord" may be wrong if it harms others in my Christian community who do not share my freedom. I want to do nothing which will hurt others or destroy the unity of our fellowship.

As a Christian I realize that God has called me to love people, not things. Not even my "right" to do something of which I honestly approve is important to me, compared to my desire to build up rather than risk tearing down other Christians.

READ

this Scripture passage.
Underline each thought here that you
recognize from the discussion on page 89.

You then, why do you judge your brother? Or why do you look down on your brother? For we will all stand before God's judgment seat. It is written:

> "'As surely as I live,' says the Lord,
> 'Every knee will bow before me;
>   every tongue will confess to God.'"

So then, each of us will give an account of himself to God.

Therefore let us stop passing judgment on one another. Instead, make up your mind not to put any stumbling block or obstacle in your brother's way. As one who is in the Lord Jesus, I am fully convinced that no food is unclean in itself. But if anyone regards something as unclean, then for him it is unclean. If your brother is distressed because of what you eat, you are no longer acting in love. Do not by your eating destroy your brother for whom Christ died. Do not allow what you consider good to be spoken of as evil. For the kingdom of God is not a matter of eating and drinking, but of righteousness, peace and joy in the Holy Spirit, because anyone who serves Christ in this way is pleasing to God and approved by men.

Let us therefore make every effort to do what leads to peace and to mutual edification. Do not destroy the work of God for the sake of food. All food is clean, but it is wrong for a man to eat anything that causes someone else to stumble. It is better not to eat meat or drink wine or to do anything else that will cause your brother to fall.

So whatever you believe about these things keep between yourself and God. Blessed is the man who does not condemn himself by what he approves. But the man who has doubts is condemned if he eats, because his eating is not from faith; and everything that does not come from faith is sin.

Romans 14:10–23

CHECK IT OUT

Think of one thing you
checked on the list on page 88
which you practice.

1 List feelings you have when you sense others' disapproval (judging).

_____

_____

_____

_____

2 List what others do that communicates disapproval (judging).

_____

_____

_____

_____

Now share your answers with each other.

TOGETHER

continue sharing in
response to *this*
question.

How has the sense of being judged affected my experience of the unity and peace of the Body?

Do what leads to peace.

READ

We are not to
judge others, but
we are to judge
our own actions.

Read aloud
each verse
on the right.
As each is read
make *personal
statements*
about how
you will apply
this truth in
your relationship
with others. Make
the statements
short and
to the point;
for example,
"I see that I need to. . . ."
or "I intend to. . . ."

Then close in prayer
that God might help each
of you *do* as He has *led.*

"I am persuaded that nothing is wrong in itself"
(Rom. 14:14 RSV).

"If your brother is distressed by what you eat you
are no longer acting in love" (Rom. 14:15).

"Let us make every effort to do what leads to peace
and mutual edification" (Rom. 14:19).

"Whatever you believe about these things keep
[them] between yourself and God" (Rom. 14:22).

"Anyone who serves Christ in this way is pleasing to
God and approved by men" (Rom. 14:18).

THIS WEEK

Each day choose one
verse of Rom. 14:10–23
for meditation.

JOURNAL

DAY 1

DAY 2

DAY 3

DAY 4

DAY 5

DAY 6

ENCOURAGEMENT

In many ways
encouragement
is the opposite
of judging.
It lets
each know that,
wherever he or she is
along the road
of commitment to Jesus,
we are
traveling the same way,
each making progress
together in
our shared journey.

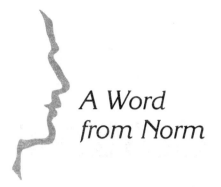

A Word from Norm

The last two studies have focused on problem situations among Christians . . . situations that can damage relationships and hinder personal growth. Most of us can recall incidents among Christians that led to injured feelings, church splits, or hostility. While the Bible is realistic about the potential for such circumstances to arise, its emphasis is on fostering positive, healthy relationships.

One means of stimulating personal growth and unity within God's family is by encouraging one another. An excellent example of this is given in Acts 18:24–28. Apollos was a zealous man with a keen mind and a love for God's Word. His public ministry was dynamic. Through the warmth and wisdom of Priscilla and Aquila he came to a clearer understanding of God's divine plan.

Apollos determined that he should go to the province of Achaia. Acts 18:27 records, "When Apollos wanted to go to Achaia, the brothers encouraged him and wrote to the disciples there to welcome him." Note the two actions by his fellow believers. First, they encouraged. They supported his decision, letting him know they believed in him and the ministry to which God had called him.

How good it is to see Christians speak well of one another. It is equally delightful to see them speak encouragingly to each other . . . building up, supporting, praising each other. One of the finest ministries we can perform to each other is the ministry of affirmation. Affirmation is telling the person of positive qualities, actions, or attitudes that we observe in him. Affirmation has incredible power to facilitate growth when shared in the environment of love.

But the Ephesian Christians did more than encourage Apollos. They expended personal effort to see that his new venture would succeed. They wrote letters to the Achaian believers to welcome Apollos. They *actively* supported his new ministry.

In a like manner we have opportunities to go beyond verbal encouragement to help others succeed. It may be writing a letter on another person's behalf, helping a friend work through the plans for a project she wants to undertake, supporting another in his first steps of ministry, providing financial resources for another, etc. Our encouragement takes a tangible form. In this way we say, "I believe in you to the extent that I will help you do that which you are called to do."

Who in your group is an Apollos, waiting to be encouraged and supported to new growth and ministry possibilities? The Scripture says that when he arrived in Achaia, "he was a great help to those who by grace had believed" (v. 27). Those who had affirmed him could rejoice in the fruit of his ministry.

Be on the lookout for your Apolloses, and encourage them.

LOOK
back and around.

Rom. 13:1–7	Rom. 13:8–14	Rom. 14:1–9	Rom. 14:10–23
SUBMISSIVE TO AUTHORITY	SHOWS LOVE TO NEIGHBORS	ACCEPTS DIFFERENCES IN OTHERS	JUDGES SELF, NOT OTHERS
_____	_____	_____	_____
_____	_____	_____	_____
_____	_____	_____	_____

For today's encouragement session, take about half your time doing the following:

1 Which of the above qualities do I admire in another member of our discipling group? Jot down name(s) in space above. Then share, telling each person listed how and why you appreciate him or her.

Then, spend the last half of your time together doing the following:

2 Identify *one* of the areas above in which you especially want to make progress.

3 Write down in that area above *what you are learning* that you want to apply. Then share your personal growth goals and what you are learning with each other.

CONCLUDE
with prayer for each other, and thanksgiving for God's work among you. This week be alert to encourage others, especially your partner. Meditate on each day's verse and let it encourage you.

JOURNAL

DAY 1   Philippians 1:16

DAY 2   2 Corinthians 3:18

DAY 3   Romans 8:29

Romans 8:16–19   **DAY 4**

1 Corinthians 2:9   **DAY 5**

1 John 3:1   **DAY 6**

WITH ONE HEART, GLORIFY GOD 10

Romans 15:1–13

The good life
calls us together
to another relationship
besides those
we've explored:
a vertical relationship.
As we grow
in freedom
to love
and support one another,
we find a fresh richness
in coming together
to worship Him.

READ

and meditate on
for three minutes.

Currents
in the Christian
life that flow to corporate worship

We who are strong ought to bear with the failings of the weak and not to please ourselves.

Romans 15:1

Each of us should please his neighbor for his good, to build him up. For even Christ did not please himself.

Romans 15:2

May the God who gives endurance and encouragement give you a spirit of unity among yourselves as you follow Christ Jesus, so that with one heart and mouth you may glorify the God and Father of our Lord Jesus Christ.

Romans 15:5

Accept one another, then, just as Christ accepted you, in order to bring praise to God.

Romans 15:7

"Therefore I will praise you among the Gentiles;
I will sing hymns to your name."

Again, it says,
"Rejoice, O Gentiles, with his people."

And again,
"Praise the Lord, all you Gentiles,
and sing praises to him, all you peoples."

And again, Isaiah says,
"The root of Jesse will spring up,
one who will arise to rule over the nations;
the Gentiles will hope in him."

May the God of hope fill you with all joy and peace
as you trust in him, so that you may overflow with
hope by the power of the Holy Spirit.

Romans 15:9–13

A Word from Larry
on Worship
Romans 15:1–13

So far in our exploration of the good life we've seen many pathways toward the deeper commitment and holiness we all yearn for. And we've learned how to take steps, together, along the path that God's Word marks out.

By His grace we have also seen growth and progress, in ourselves and in each other. That is what the encouragement session last week was designed to point out. That God *has* been at work in us. That there is much hope and encouragement for us because of His good work.

Also the encouragement session was designed to help us draw closer to each other by affirming one another. Affirming means point out and express appreciation for the good things we see God doing in one another. It is pleasing to God to recognize His work in His disciples, and encouraging when we tell each other that we are pleased with their progress.

Stop for just a moment, and think of things others said about you and your growth. Jot down a phrase or two that someone used that was particularly encouraging for you.

_____

_____

Now, before you go on, express to God your appreciation for His encouragement of you through your brothers and sisters.

Affirmation is, surprisingly, quite close to worship. The two are alike in that worship involves focusing on something you appreciate—some good thing you see God doing. The two are different in that while affirmation of a brother involves speaking to him, worship involves us in direct address to God.

Worship is not talking about God to others. It is not even speaking to God about others. Worship, in the sense of Romans 15:9 as "glorifying God" is speaking directly to Him to tell Him, in prayer, in praise, in songs, in Scripture, how wonderful *He* is.

And what are the things for which His people come together to praise God? Romans 13 suggests two of the many. First, there is praise for the work He has been doing in us to bring us, together, to a unity enriched by our common commitment to His way, the good life (13:1, 2, 5, 7). Second, there is the fact that in living the good life we are simply following Jesus, who has come this way before.

Thus Paul writes that "even Christ did not please himself," and that "Christ has become a servant" so that Jew and Gentile may experience and glorify God for His mercy.

In this session of growing together into deeper discipleship, there's no need to *talk* about worship. Instead, we suggest you spend the bulk of your time together in worshiping and affirming the Lord, telling Him how pleased and thankful and full of praise you are for His great gift of Jesus, and His gift of growth in goodness in each of your lives.

Before turning to the next page, which will help you prepare for meaningful worship together, consider again: What is it you have seen God doing in the lives of others in the group—and in your own life—for which He merits praise? What is it about Jesus that, right now, fills your heart with appreciation?

PREPARE FOR WORSHIP

Spend about
ten minutes
in personal meditation
and in preparation
for worship.

What is it you would like to express to God, and lead the others to say to Him?

What is the most appropriate form for this expression?

A Prayer?
A song?
A hymn?
A psalm?
A personal psalm you write?

In the space to the right write your own expression of praise to God, selecting any of these forms.

Then, when everyone is prepared, lead each other in unity to bring your shared praise to the Lord.

Praise

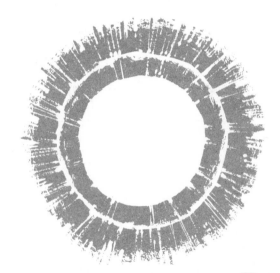

THIS WEEK

Search out a
different psalm each
day that expresses
your own praise
and "pray" it
to the Lord.

Journal

Search out a different psalm each day that expresses your own praise and "pray" it to the Lord.

DAY 1

DAY 2

DAY 3

DAY 4

DAY 5

DAY 6

111

A PERSONAL MINISTRY FOR ALL

Romans 15:14–33

One exciting discovery
we make
in living the good life
is about ourselves.
And about
our calling
to active ministry
in Jesus' kingdom.
In this session
we take
a close look—*at* you,
and *around* you.

VISIT
a house
of mirrors.

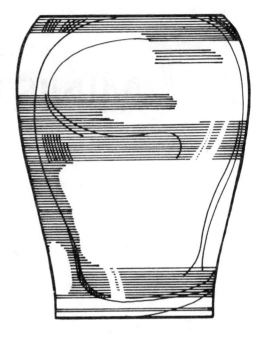

With your partner, look at each of these mirrors; tell your partner and then jot down words that describe how you—or others—have tended to see you.

As a teenager,
I saw myself as

_____

_____

_____

_____

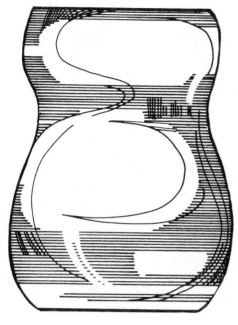

When I was in
my early twenties,
my parents saw me
as

_____

_____

_____

_____

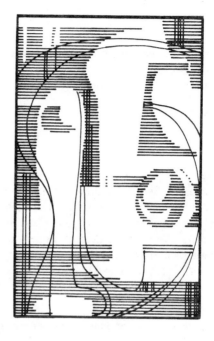

Right now there
are people who
see me as

_____

_____

_____

_____

A TRUE MIRROR

I myself am convinced, my brothers, that you yourselves are full of goodness, complete in knowledge
and competent to instruct one another.

Romans 15:14

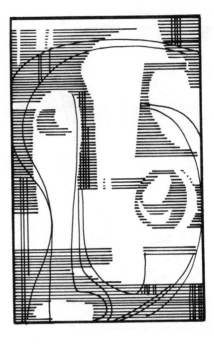

How does
God view
you now?

These words of Scripture, drawn from Romans
15:14, point up an important truth. All of us as we
have grown have learned to see ourselves in dis-
torted mirrors. We have pictures of ourselves, and
others have pictures of us, which are not in harmony with the reality of who we are *now* in Christ.
Nor are they in harmony with who we are becoming.

Learning to live God's good life involves coming to
understand the new persons we are, and learning
to act out of our new identity rather than out of the
old one.

We may have been inadequate before, and our
parents may have been disappointed in us. Or sure
that we would never be able to succeed.

But now God speaks to us through the apostle Paul
and says we *are* competent. In Jesus we are full of
goodness. We are complete in knowledge—we
have all we need to know God's will. And we are
competent to instruct each other. *You,* and I, are
able to minister and to serve!

READ

In Romans 15:15–33 Paul describes his personal ministry, evangelism, and shows confidence in his readers by inviting them to participate with him. Read the passage and circle sections, as shown.

I have written you quite boldly on some points, as if to remind you of them again, because of the grace God gave me to be a minister of Christ Jesus to the Gentiles with the priestly duty of proclaiming the gospel of God, so that the Gentiles might become an offering acceptable to God, sanctified by the Holy Spirit.

Paul defines his ministry.

Therefore I glory in Christ Jesus in my service to God. I will not venture to speak of anything except what Christ has accomplished through me in leading the Gentiles to obey God by what I have said and done—by the power of signs and miracles, through the power of the Spirit. So from Jerusalem all the way around to Illyricum, I have fully proclaimed the gospel of Christ. It has always been my ambition to preach the gospel where Christ was not known, so that I would not be building on someone else's foundation. Rather, as it is written:

Paul shares his goals.

> "Those who were not told about him will see,
> and those who have not heard will understand."

This is why I have often been hindered from coming to you.

But now that there is no more place for me to work in these regions, and since I have been longing for many years to see you, I plan to do so when I go to Spain. I hope to visit you while passing through and to have you assist me on my journey there, after I have enjoyed your company for a while. Now, however, I am on my way to Jerusalem in the service of the saints there. For Macedonia and Achaia were pleased to make a contribution for the poor among the saints in Jerusalem. They were pleased to do it, and indeed they owe it to them. For if the Gentiles have shared in the Jews' spiritual blessings, they owe it to the Jews to share with them their material blessings. So after I have completed this task and have made sure that they have received this fruit, I will go to Spain and visit you on the way. I know that when I come to you, I will come in the full measure of the blessing of Christ.

Paul shares his schedule.

I urge you, brothers, by our Lord Jesus Christ and by the love of the Spirit, to join me in my struggle by praying to God for me. Pray that I may be rescued from the unbelievers in Judea and that my service in Jerusalem may be acceptable to the saints there, so that by God's will I may come to you with joy and together with you be refreshed. The God of peace be with you all. Amen.

Paul shares his prayer requests.

Romans 15:15–33

DEFINITIONS

"Personal
Ministry"

Any way in which I can serve or help another person in a material, social, or spiritual way as an expression of Jesus' love.

"Goals"

Specific plans or intents to minister to others.

"Schedule"

Ways in which my plans for ministry will be carried out in the next week or so.

"Prayer Requests"

Needs for God's supply or enablement to help me reach ministry goals or achieve a schedule which I am aware of now.

ACTION

Complete as full a description as you can of your own personal ministry, using the definition on p. 119. And fill in the other spaces with goals, schedule and prayer requests.

MY PERSONAL MINISTRY

_____

_____

_____

MINISTRY GOALS

_____

_____

_____

MINISTRY SCHEDULE

_____

_____

_____

PRAYER REQUESTS

_____

_____

_____

SHARE

with each other your own
ministry, your goals, your
schedule, and prayer
requests.

Meet as an entire group or
in sixes for this sharing.
Spend the rest of this
time together in mutual sharing
and in prayer.

THIS WEEK

Be alert this week
for ways to express
who you are in Christ
in ministry to others
and share goals,
schedules, and
requests with your partner.

JOURNAL

DAY 1

DAY 2

DAY 3

DAY 4

DAY 5

DAY 6

123

FELLOWSHIP OF COMMITMENT 12

Romans 16

God's good life,
as we have seen,
is not an individualistic experience.
Instead God's call
to the good life draws us
into fellowship with others
who are committed
to love and follow Him.
Even as great an individual
as Paul the apostle
reveals the joys
awaiting you and me
in relationships.

READ CAREFULLY

The twin themes of fellowship
and shared commitment
are both reflected in
the final chapter of
the letter to the Romans.
Read, and complete together
the chart on page 128
by recording every significant
observation you can discover.
Sample observations are
included to help you begin.

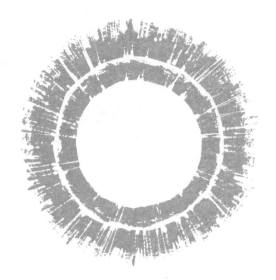

I commend to you our sister Phoebe, a servant of the church in Cenchrea. I ask you to receive her in the Lord in a way worthy of the saints and to give her any help she may need from you, for she has been a great help to many people, including me.

Greet Priscilla and Aquila, my fellow workers in Christ Jesus. They risked their lives for me. Not only I but all the churches of the Gentiles are grateful to them.

Greet also the church that meets at their house.

Greet my dear friend Epenetus, who was the first convert to Christ in the province of Asia.

Greet Mary, who worked very hard for you.

Greet Andronicus and Junias, my relatives who have been in prison with me.

They are outstanding among the apostles, and they were in Christ before I was.

Greet Ampliatus, whom I love in the Lord.

Greet Urbanus, our fellow worker in Christ, and my dear friend Stachys.

Greet Apelles, tested and approved in Christ.

Greet those who belong to the household of Aristobulus.

Greet Herodion, my relative.

Greet those in the household of Narcissus who are in the Lord.

Greet Tryphena and Tryphosa, those women who work hard in the Lord.

Greet my dear friend Persis, another woman who has worked very hard in the Lord.

Greet Rufus, chosen in the Lord, and his mother, who has been a mother to me, too.

Greet Asyncritus, Phlegon, Hermes, Patrobas, Hermas and the brothers with them.

Greet Philologus, Julia, Nereus and his sister, and Olympas and all the saints with them.

Greet one another with a holy kiss.

All the churches of Christ send greetings.

I urge you, brothers, to watch out for those who cause divisions and put obstacles in your way that are contrary to the teaching you have learned. Keep away from them. For such people are not serving our Lord Christ, but their own appetites. By smooth talk and flattery they deceive the minds of naive people. Everyone has heard about your obedience, so I am full of joy over you; but I want you to be wise about what is good, and innocent about what is evil.

The God of peace will soon crush Satan under your feet.

The grace of our Lord Jesus be with you.

Timothy, my fellow worker, sends his greetings to you, as do Lucius, Jason and Sosipater, my relatives.

I, Tertius, who wrote down this letter, greet you in the Lord.

Gaius, whose hospitality I and the whole church here enjoy, sends you his greetings.

Erastus, who is the city's director of public works, and our brother Quartus send you their greetings.

Romans 16:1–23

FELLOWSHIP	COMMITMENT
men and women mentioned social distances (slaves to city planners: vs. 23) are bridged	women are given recognition as fellow workers

A Word from Norm

Read aloud to the group

The Good Life Reproduces Itself.

The good life rarely flourishes in isolation. God is able to meet the needs of those who are forced to live alone. His plan, however, is for His people to be knit together in healthy relationships which nurture growth. Romans 16 is a vivid expression of shared life among Christians.

As Paul expresses his heartfelt feeling for the Romans, he portrays individuals who are experiencing the good life and reproducing themselves in others. He also gives us a model of the nurturing environment. We can perceive several ingredients which allow the abundant life to flourish.

We note a climate of *loving relationships.* A sense of warmth and care permeates the entire chapter. Paul's fondness for individuals breaks through repeatedly. These are people whom Paul loves and who love each other.

A strong sense of *shared life* is apparent. He identifies those who were fellow workers, those who endured prison with him, those who were a part of a household. They did not merely attend meetings weekly, but involved themselves in each other's lives in times of joy and hardship. I am reminded of Luke's description of the early Christians: "They broke bread in their homes and ate together with glad and sincere hearts . . ." (Acts 2:46).

Another ingredient we observe is a *respect for the uniqueness of individuals* . . . without stereotyping or demeaning people. Men and women shared a mutual ministry. Each was esteemed highly for the special contribution he or she made to the Body of Christ. Paul begins by commending a lady who obviously had a significant ministry. Then he asks others (men included) to support her in this good work.

Within the Roman church Christians shared the good life *without a sense of social class.* Rich and poor found a oneness in Christ. Paul sends greetings from Erastus, who held a position as director of public works. He shared his life with the poor, the slaves, the uneducated.

Within the nurturing environment we notice people who are *committed to serve each other.* The commitment apparently had come from within . . . motivated by the Spirit's love. Some were willing to risk their lives for Paul (v. 4). Others opened their homes so that friends could gather with them for prayer, praise, and encouragement. Several individuals are identified as having worked hard for the Lord and fellow believers.

This final chapter of Romans has a powerful message for us. The example of individuals' lives speaks powerfully . . . the testimony of God's people loving, serving, and supporting each other. What a portrait of the good life!

Continuum Study

Look at this discipling group of which you are a part. On a scale of 1 to 10, where are you in the process of becoming a fellowship of commitment?

Mark the continuum with a check (√).

A FELLOWSHIP OF COMMITMENT

1 ————————————————————————————— 10

Share

Compare your evaluations, and briefly share why you each marked as you did.

RECORD

evaluations of others in your group.
What strengths and weaknesses were observed?

_____

_____

_____

_____

_____

_____

_____

_____

_____

_____

_____

_____

_____

ACTION PLAN

List *two specific* ways you can contribute toward movement along the continuum to a more matured fellowship of commitment—toward God's ideal.

1 _____

2 _____

Finally, share your action plans as a commitment to the others . . . and together close in prayer.

THIS WEEK

Seek ways this week to deepen your fellowship with your partner or others in the group.

JOURNAL

_____

DAY 1

_____

DAY 2

_____

DAY 3

DAY 4

DAY 5

DAY 6

A FINAL ENCOURAGEMENT 13

In pursuing
God's good life you
have grown together
toward His fellowship
of commitment;
His new community
of serving love.
Recognize His work
and be glad!

REMEMBER
the continuum
from last session?

A FELLOWSHIP OF COMMITMENT

1 _____ 10

Put the check mark (√) along the continuum in the *same place* you put it last week.

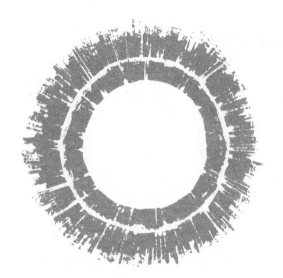

Focus

Often in using a continuum chart, we focus on what *has not yet been achieved.* Last week that part of the continuum to the right of your check mark *was* the focus of your time together. For this final encouragement time, however, you will focus together on the part of the continuum to the *left* of your check.

You will focus on the growth toward a committed fellowship which *has* taken place.

Individually List

1 What good things in your experience in this group indicate to you that you have made progress toward becoming a good life fellowship?

_____

_____

_____

_____

_____

_____

2 In what specific ways have individuals made distinctive contributions toward this growth? List names and individual contributions.

_____

_____

_____

_____

_____

_____

_____

_____

SHARE

Take turns sitting
in the center of a circle.

Let everyone share a way in which the
center person contributes to the growth of
a "fellowship of commitment."

Then pray together with thanksgiving.

THE GOOD LIFE: A SUMMARY

12:1–2   Transformed by God's work in us, we are to prove (discover by experience) that God's will for us is good—and that the good is acceptable and perfect.

12:3–13   God's "good and acceptable and perfect" will for His transformed people brings us into a *Body* relationship with each other, in which we love our brothers and sisters and serve each other with our gifts.

12:14–21   Sharing life harmoniously and harmlessly teaches us how to grow and how to "overcome evil with good."

Romans

13:1–7   Goodness in our relationship with society means to live in submission to human governments and institutions.

13:8–14   Goodness in our relationship with non-Christians means to love our neighbor and have whole-hearted commitment to a holy life.

14:1–9   Goodness in our relationship with our brothers and sisters in Christ means to welcome them and accept them in spite of differences.

14:10–23   Goodness in our relationship with our brothers and sisters in Christ means not judging them, but learning how to judge our own actions by seeing how they affect others.

15:1–13   Goodness in our relationship with our brothers and sisters in Christ means building them up and working together toward a unity within which we together praise God.

15:14–33   Being "full of goodness" involves exercising our priestly ministries and reaching out for universal fellowship with all the saints.

16:1–27   Goodness is demonstrated in the beauty of the relationships between the saints which Paul's final greetings reveal.